LESSON 3

Play the following:

Roller Coaster

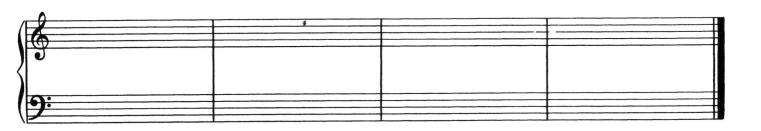

Now with the same notes:

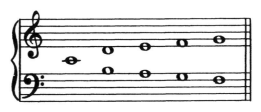

. . . compose (play and write) your own ending to "Roller Coaster", using any combination of:

♩ (quarter note)

♩ (half note)

○ (whole note)

After you have completed this assignment, play the entire composition.

REPETITION AND SEQUENCE

LESSON 4

Repetition and *Sequence* are used in many musical compositions.

Repetition means to repeat a motive (a musical theme) — note for note — starting on the same pitch.

Example: (Play)

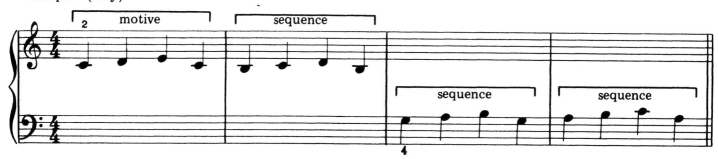

Sequence means to repeat a motive starting on any *different* pitch.

Example: (Play)

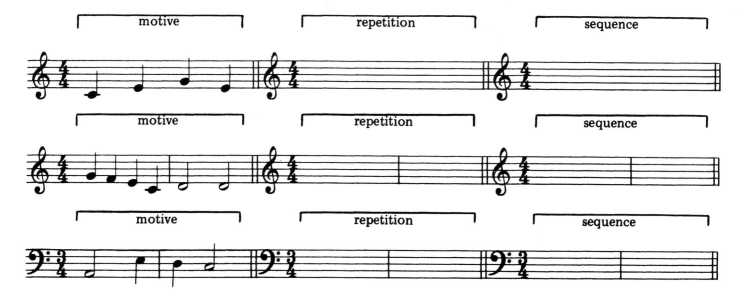

Note to the teacher   Sequences may be constructed in two ways:

① by utilizing white keys only, without regard to the exact intervals of the given motive, or

② by duplicating the exact interval relationship of the given motive.

EXERCISES

Write a repetition and sequence of each of the following motives:

Learn to COMPOSE and NOTATE MUSIC at the Keyboard
Beginning Level

LEE EVANS   MARTHA BAKER
PIANO
FUNCTIONAL SKILLS SERIES

CONTENTS

3rd Edition

Music Engravings and Typography by
Irwin Rabinowitz

Piano Plus, inc.

EXCLUSIVELY DISTRIBUTED BY

HAL•LEONARD® CORPORATION
7777 W. BLUEMOUND RD. P.O. BOX 13819 MILWAUKEE, WI 53213

INTRODUCTION

The authors strongly believe that to achieve comprehensive musicianship more effectively and rapidly, all piano students should know how to notate music... and should therefore be given writing assignments at every lesson.
A creative approach to the learning of writing skills will involve pupils in the activity of composing. This volume introduces fundamental compositional techniques — repetition, sequence, retrograde, and inversion — to the early level student.

All exercises should be played as well as written. When written, the teacher should instruct the student in such basics as stem directions (all stems down from the third staff line and above — all stems approximately one octave in length), the correct shape of rests, and the entering of dynamic and tempo markings in each piece where appropriate. The authors suggest limiting dynamic and tempo markings to a selected few for this level. A list of such recommended terms appears in the Glossary on page 24.

The authors recommend that students be required to enter rests in each measure wherever necessary.

Examples:

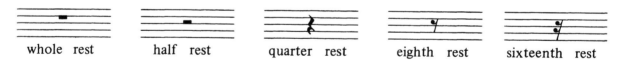

| whole rest | half rest | quarter rest | eighth rest | sixteenth rest |

JUST TO GET STARTED. . .

LESSON 1

Play the following:

The Woodpecker

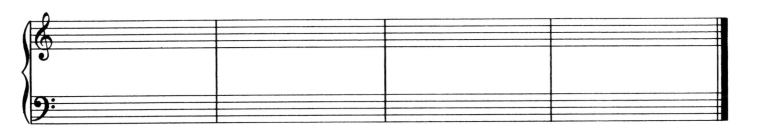

Now, with the same notes (G and C) — in any octave — compose (play and write) your own ending to "The Woodpecker", using any combination of:

♩ (quarter note)

♩ (half note)

𝅝 (whole note)

Note: It is not absolutely necessary to end your compositions on the tonic tone, but doing so will give your endings a more final sound.

After you have completed this assignment, play the entire composition.

LET'S DO ANOTHER. . .

LESSON 2

Play the following:

Skating

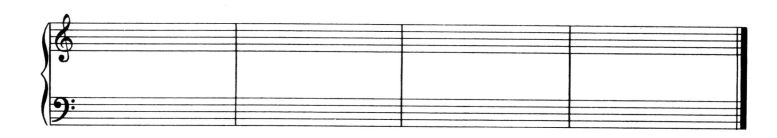

Now, with the same notes — F, G, C and D — compose (play and write) your own ending to "Skating", using any combination of:

♩ (quarter note)

♩ (half note)

♩. (dotted half note)

Note: The tonic tone of the above composition is F.   Ending on F will therefore make this piece sound more final.

After you have completed this assignment, play the entire composition.

COMPOSING: REPETITION AND SEQUENCE

LESSON 5

Use repetition and sequence to compose (play and write) the remainder of the following piece:

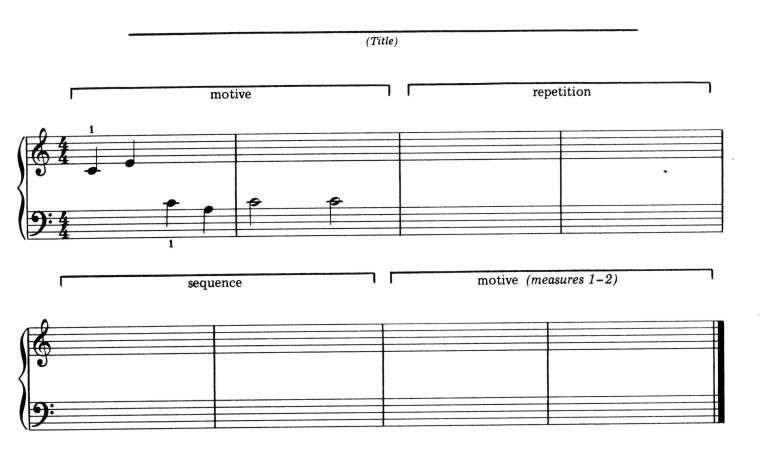

Give your composition a title in the space above.

(Practice your composition as part of your regular piano practice.)

COMPOSING: REPETITION AND SEQUENCE

LESSON 6

Compose (play and write) another piece using repetition and sequence, based on the motive provided in the first two measures.

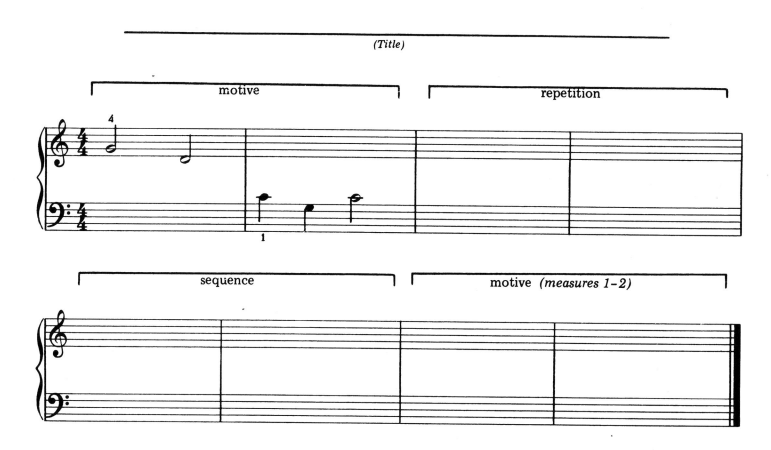

Give your composition a title in the space above.

(Practice your composition as part of your regular piano practice.)

COMPOSING: REPETITION AND SEQUENCE

LESSON 7

Compose (play and write) your own 2 measure motive; then use repetition and sequence to complete the piece. (Suggestion: for variety, consider using some staccato notes.)

_____
(Title)

motive | repetition

sequence | motive (measures 1-2)

Give your composition a title in the space above.

(Practice your composition as part of your regular piano practice.)

PP-2

RETROGRADE

LESSON 8

Retrograde is also used in many musical compositions.

| Retrograde | means to play the notes of a motive backwards. While retrogrades may occur in any rhythm, in this book make all retrogrades appear in the same rhythm as the original motive appears forwards. This will make the motive and retrograde sound more unified (fit together better).

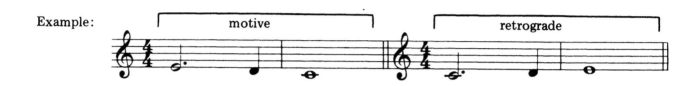

EXERCISES

Write a retrograde of each of the following motives:

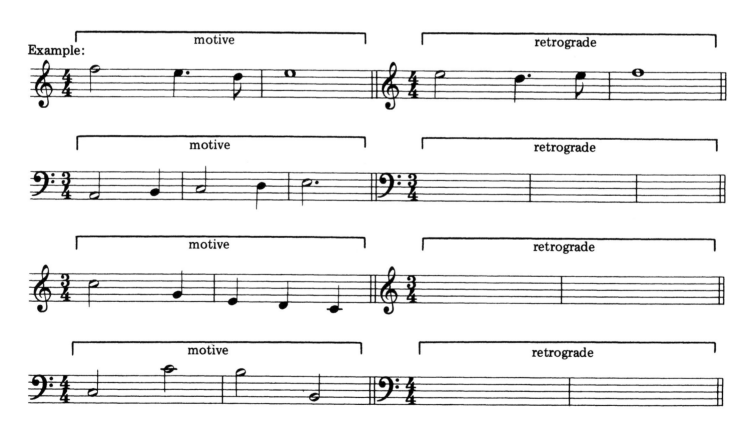

COMPOSING: RETROGRADE

LESSON 9

Compose (play and write) music in the blank measures (measures 4, 6, 8) according to the directions given in each of those measures, being sure to use phrasing and articulation marks (i.e., staccatos, etc.) as they appear in the given motives. Continue to do so in the remaining compositions of this book.

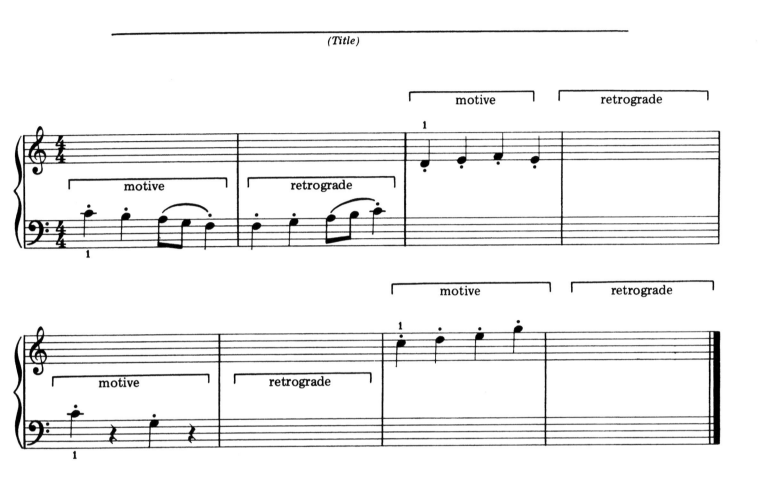

(Title)

Give your composition a title in the space above.

(Practice your composition as part of your regular piano practice.)

COMPOSING: RETROGRADE

LESSON 10

Compose (play and write) music in the blank measures according to the directions given in each of those measures:

_____

(Title)

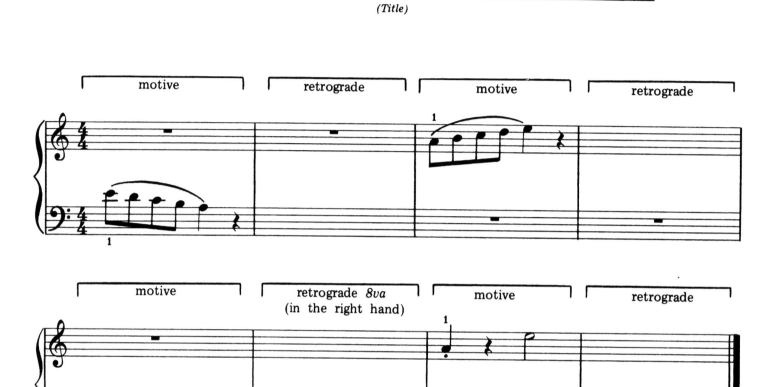

Give your composition a title in the space above.

(Practice your composition as part of your regular piano practice.)

COMPOSING: REPETITION, SEQUENCE, RETROGRADE

LESSON 11

Now compose (play and write) music using all three compositional devices —

repetition, *sequence* and *retrograde*.

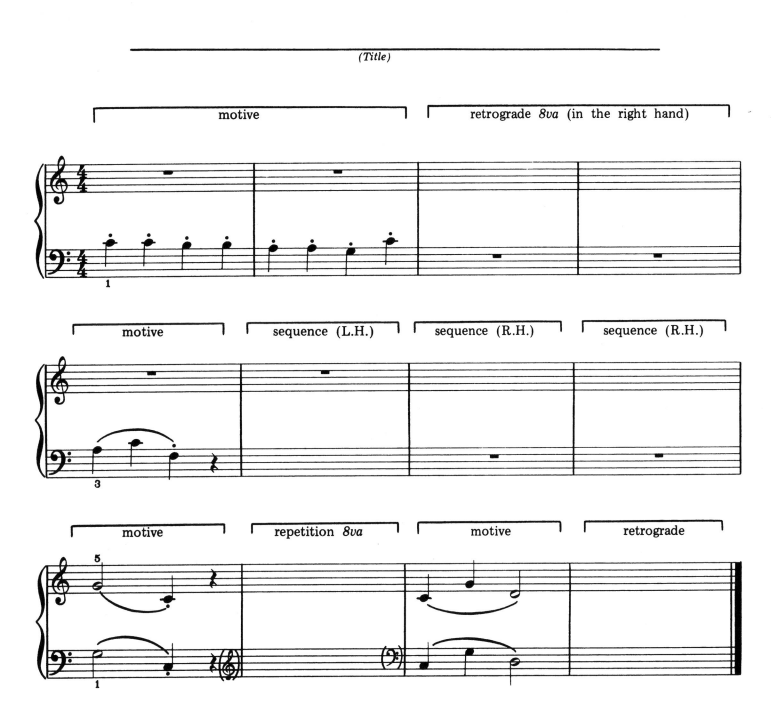

(Title)

Give your composition a title in the space above.

(Practice your composition as part of your regular piano practice.)

COMPOSING: REPETITION, SEQUENCE, RETROGRADE

LESSON 12

Compose (play and write) another piece using all three compositional devices we have learned — *repetition*, *sequence* and *retrograde*.

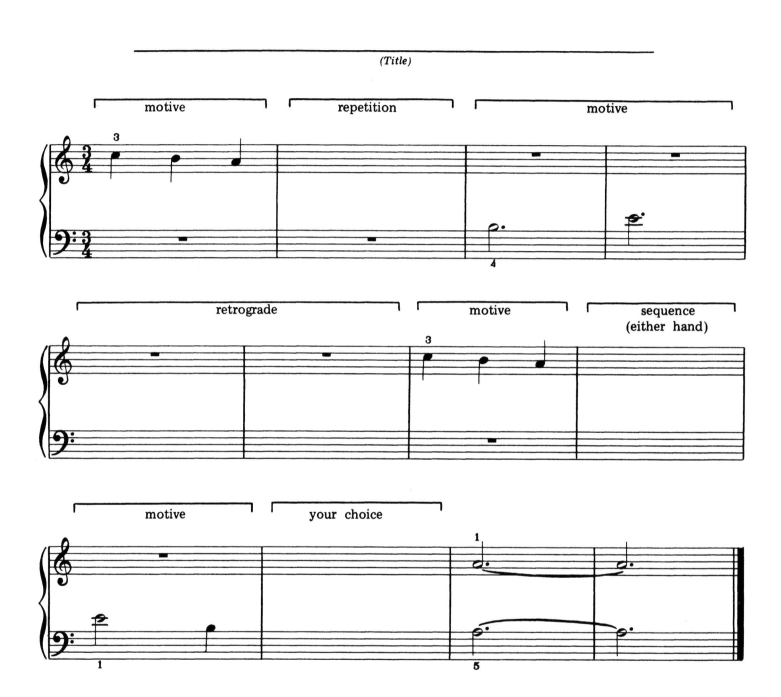

(Title)

Give your composition a title in the space above.

(Practice your composition as part of your regular piano practice.)

COMPOSING: REPETITION, SEQUENCE, RETROGRADE

LESSON 13

Compose (play and write) your own original composition using *repetition*, *sequence* and *retrograde*. Make the piece 12 measures long, four measures on each line. For your composition to be as complete as possible, you will also need to:

— — add clef signs;

— — choose a time signature;

— — draw bar lines as needed;

— — add a tempo-marking and dynamics (see page 24.)

_____

(Title)

Give your composition a title in the space above.

(Practice your composition as part of your regular piano practice.)

INVERSION

LESSON 14

Still another compositional device is *inversion.*

| Inversion | means to play the intervals of a motive upside down (in mirror image.)

For example, if in a motive an interval goes *up* a perfect 4th, then to invert it go *down* a perfect 4th.

If in the motive an interval goes *down* a perfect 5th, then to invert it go *up* a perfect 5th. And so on. . .

Here are some musical examples of inversions:

Examples:

In each of the above examples the inversion started on the same note as the motive.

But inversion may also start on any other note as well:

Example:

EXERCISES

Invert the following motives:

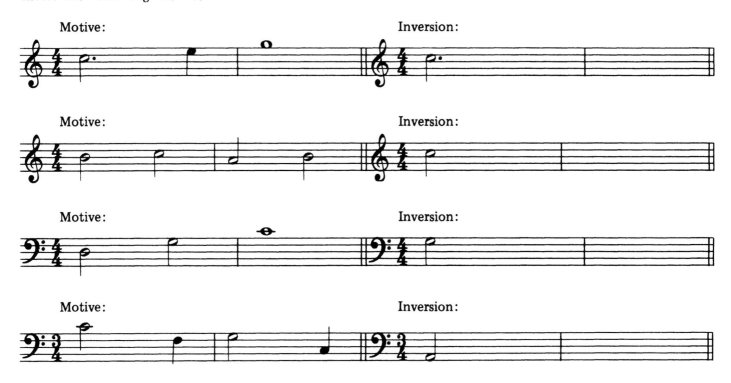

MORE INVERSION EXERCISES

LESSON 15

COMPOSING: INVERSION

LESSON 16

Now use inversion to compose (play and write) the remainder of the following piece:

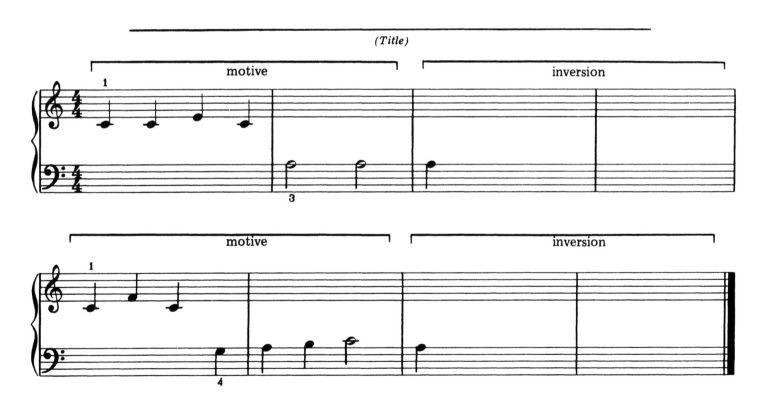

Give your composition a title in the space above.

(Practice your composition as part of your regular piano practice.)

REVIEW

(Everything Exercises)

Repetition: Sequence: Another sequence:

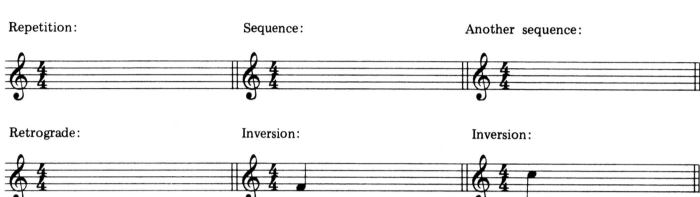

Retrograde: Inversion: Inversion:

Repetition: Sequence: Another sequence:

Retrograde: Inversion: Inversion:

MORE REVIEW

(Everything Exercises)

LESSON 18

Motive:

Repetition: Sequence: Another sequence:

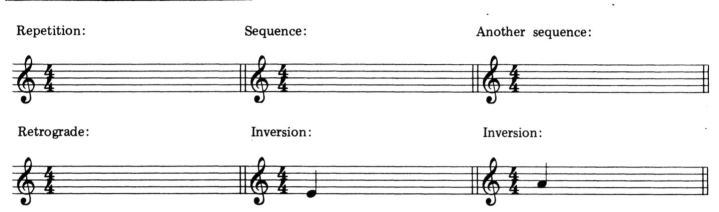

Retrograde: Inversion: Inversion:

Motive:

Repetition: Sequence: Another sequence:

Retrograde: Inversion: Inversion:

PP-2

COMPOSITIONAL ROUNDUP

LESSON 19

Compose a piece of any length using compositional devices you have learned in this book, plus any others with which you may wish to experiment. Some *new* compositional devices are explained and illustrated in the Appendix on pages 22 and 23.*

First draw grand staffs, clefs and time signature. Add bar lines as needed, placing a double bar at the end of the composition. Include dynamics and tempo-markings.

_____

(Title)

---

* | Note to the teacher | Selected compositional devices from the Appendix on pages 22 and 23 are taught at a slower pace in the follow-up volume, "COMPOSING AT THE PIANO."

COMPOSITIONAL ROUNDUP

LESSON 20

Compose another piece of any length using compositional devices you have learned in this book, plus any others with which you may wish to experiment. (See Appendix on pages 22 and 23.)

First draw grand staffs, clefs and time signature. Add bar lines as needed, placing a double bar at the end of the composition. Include dynamics and tempo-markings.

_____

(Title)

PP-2 You are now ready to proceed to "COMPOSING AT THE PIANO" (Early Intermediate Level).

APPENDIX

REPETITION AND SEQUENCE IN ALTERED FORMS

Sequence is not always an exact repetition of a motive at another scale degree.

Sequences may appear in *altered* forms such as:

Activity	(Name of Activity)	Example

Smaller Rhythms   *(Rhythmic Diminution)*

The melody stays the same, but note values become smaller.

Larger Rhythms   *(Rhythmic Augmentation)*

The melody stays the same, but note values become larger.

Smaller Intervals   *(Intervallic Diminution)*

The rhythm stays the same, but melodic intervals become smaller.

Larger Intervals   *(Intervallic Augmentation)*

The rhythm stays the same, but melodic intervals become larger.

Part of a motive   *(Fragmentation)*

Only a portion of a motive (rather than the entire motive) is treated in sequence or repetition.

Note: The material of this Appendix is excerpted from Lee Evans' volume, *Improvise By Learning How To Compose.*

Complete change of melody (Complete Melodic Alteration)

The rhythm stays the same, but all pitch relationships change.

Rhythm shift   (Rhythmic shift)

The melody and note values stay the same, but occur on different beats of the measure.

Octave shift   (Octave Displacement)

A note or motive played an octave higher or lower in repetition or sequence.

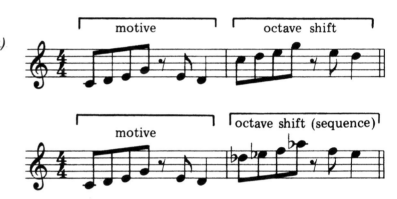

In the following example, many of these are combined:

Example:

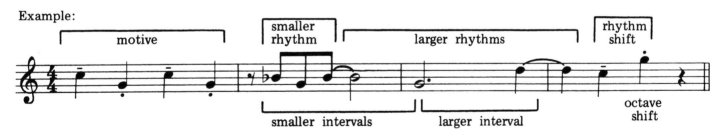

PP-2

GLOSSARY

Dynamic Markings:

Abbreviation	*Italian*	*Definition*
pp	pianissimo	very soft
p	piano	soft
mf	mezzo forte	medium loud
f	forte	loud
>	——	accent
crescendo sign	crescendo	gradually louder
diminuendo sign	diminuendo (decrescendo)	gradually softer

Tempo Markings:

Italian	*Definition*
Lento	slow
Andante	medium slow
Moderato	a medium tempo
Allegro	medium fast; happy
Vivace	fast; lively

Dynamics and tempo marks are usually placed as follows: